CHANGE YOUR WORDS CHANGE YOUR LIFE

The book on being grateful, connected and inspired

DAVID PRIOR

WOW Book Publishing™

First Edition Published by David Prior
Copyright ©2021 David Prior
ISBN: 979-8717177580
WOW Book Publishing™

All rights reserved. Neither this book, nor any parts within it may be sold or reproduced in any form without permission. No part of this book may be reproduced in any form or by any electronic or mechanical means including information storage and retrieval systems, without permission in writing from the author. The only exception is by a reviewer, who may quote short excerpts in a review.

The purpose of this book is to educate and entertain. The views and opinions expressed in this book are that of the author based on his personal experiences and education. The author does not guarantee that anyone following the techniques, suggestions, ideas or strategies will become successful.

The author shall neither be liable nor responsible for any loss or damage allegedly arising from any information or suggestion in this book.

Warning - Disclaimer

The reason for this book is to provide information to help educate and to entertain, neither the author, nor the publisher guarantee that the suggestions and techniques will be successful. In this case therefore neither the Author nor the Publisher will have any responsibility nor liability for any loss or damage which may be caused either directly or indirectly by the information in this book.

Dedication

In loving Memory of my late sister Phyllis Clarke, I dedicate this book to her as a thank you for all her love and support throughout the years.

I also dedicate this book to Erica, who has been a special friend to me for ten years and has helped me with this book.

I also dedicate this book to you, the reader.

I hope that it will inspire you and help you on your ever evolving journey to become more successful in all that you do.

A Poem for the Reader

I AM

I am here to help you, I am here to give

It's my purpose for being here, It's my purpose to live.

I am now living in the present time,

I am feeling well again, I am feeling fine,

I am enjoying the sunshine, but we need the rain, I am here to appreciate and not be vain.

I am here to learn about how to love, I am here to study and rise above,

The challenges that try to get in my way, But by never giving up I can win the day.

Table of Contents

Dedication 3
A Poem for the Reader 5
   I AM 5
Table of Contents 7
Acknowledgements 9
Testimonials 11
Foreword 13
About the Author 15
BEAUTIFUL MOMENTS 17
The Magic of Thinking Big 19
   Pause 27
   THE HEART OF THE MATTER 31
The Power of the Written and Spoken Word 33
   Activity 1 35
   Words 37
The Power of Belief 39
   Activity 2 41
The Power of Gratitude 47
   The Magic of Gratitude 49
   I am Grateful 50
   THE MOON AND THE STARS 51
   REMEMBER 52
   A JOURNAL OF GRATITUDE 53
   Activity 3 54
   Combined activity 55
The Importance of Self-esteem 57
   I am enough 58
   Combined activity 61
   Self-Confidence 63

Table of Contents

Changing Your Thoughts 65
WHO'S PERFECT ANYWAY 66
Activity 4 67
The Value of Forgiveness 71
Benefiting from Forgiveness 73
Activity 5 74
Vibrational Levels 77
A Note on Self-development Experts 81
A Few More Poems to Keep you Inspired 83
BE HAPPY NOW 83
Special moments 84
LOOKING ON THE BRIGHT SIDE OF LIFE 85
THE BLESSING 86
HAPPINESS 87
THE BEST MEDICINE 88
The Key To Happiness 89
Other Poems 91
THE JOURNEY 91
IS THIS JUST ME 93
THE GAME OF LIFE 94
BEING GRATEFUL. 95
PENCIL POWER. 96
BUFFY. 97
KINDNESS 98
Ho'oponopono 99
Ho'oponopono - Blue Water 103
Ho'oponopono 105

Acknowledgements

I acknowledge that there are many great motivators in the world of self-development.

I acknowledge the wonderful individuals who have now passed on who have made major contributions to the world of the self-development field, such as Louise Hay, Wayne Dyer, Earl Nightingale, Napoleon Hill, Zig Ziglar, Steven Covey, Dale Carnegie and many more.

I would also like to acknowledge some of the current motivational experts, all of whom I have carried out online courses with, and in the case of Marisa Peer, I attended one of her live seminars, which I refer to in my book.

They have all made a unique contribution in helping and changing and improving people's lives, and I have learnt so much from every one of them.

They are: Lisa Nichols, Marisa Peer, Natalie Ledwell, Joe Vitale, Sonia Ricotti, Vishen Lakhaini and Jim Katsulis.

Acknowledgements

I would like to acknowledge my late sister who passed away on the 20th of January 2019. She had a heart of gold, and was the most loving person I ever knew. We did have our differences, but we always loved and supported each other, and if she had been here today, she would have been really proud of my efforts in writing this book.

Phyllis is greatly missed by myself as well as by Erica, who used to look after Phyllis. Phyllis and Erica got on so well together that they were almost like mother and daughter. We spent many happy hours together listening to music, visiting places, and watching films and DVDs, and we loved every minute of it.

I would also like to acknowledge Erica, My special friend as we both have health issues and I would like to thank her for all the guidance and advice she has given me over the years.

Testimonials

"I have known David Prior for over twenty years as a much respected individual and a Trustee of Manchester Carers Centre. David has always offered me invaluable support and advice in my role as a CEO. David has infinite positivity and is a real encourager. His book reflects his philosophy, knowledge and wisdom obtained from overcoming many challenges in his own life. David is inspirational and a wonderful human being and I commend his book to you as a fantastic tool to help you navigate the ups and downs of life."

— Shirley Devine

"I have known David for over ten years, and I have always been grateful for the advice and help he has given me. He has helped me look at life in a more positive manner, and he has been like a father figure to me. I am sure his book will help a lot of people see the benefits of focusing their attention in looking for the good in all that they do."

— Moupiya Shilpi Sanyal
Senior Customer Service Executive

Testimonials

"David attends our church here at St. Michael's, Middleton, Manchester, but has not been able to attend recently, due to Covid 19 restrictions. I enjoy reading the inspiring poetry he writes, his positive outlook on life, and the hope he instills. I am sure the contents of his book will help many people to look at life in a more positive manner."

—**The Rev. Jackie Calow, Former Vicar, St. Michael's, Tonge-cum- Alkrington, and also All Saints, Rhodes,**
The New Vicarage, Boardman Lane, Rhodes, Middleton, Manchester, United Kingdom.

"We have been friends since childhood, David is always willing to give advice which is has been a real help to me. He always looks at the bright side of life in everything he does. This book should help and inspire people whatever their age. I'm really look forward to reading it."

—**Paul Dodge**
Former resources manager in the railway control office.

Foreword

David is an amazing author, he is very inspirational. With his book, he shares the tips and teachings of the gurus who have both helped and inspired him in life. Being well-versed in and working with many self-development programmes throughout his life, David shares with us those which have been the most effective.

Moreover, with his unique and most inspiring poetry, I know that he will help all who read this book to find balance in their lives. His simple activities, tips and tricks will not only help you start your journey of self-development but also help you keep on track with your daily and weekly progress.

—Vishal Morjaria
Award Winning Author
and International Speaker

About the Author

David Prior has been blessed with a long life filled with gratitude and bliss this is because of having an illness so severe at the age of four; that he almost died. The doctors said that him surviving was a true miracle and because of that David has seen the world differently ever since. It has given him a greater understanding and clarity as well as a personal insight into the philosophy of taking one day at a time because he knows very well that all his life has been a blessing which he came so close to not having.

David's life has had its ups and downs, and he has had his own share of suffering; however, with his outlook on life, not only is he always the helper, but he is truly empathetic to those in need. He views himself more as an observer of life rather than a participant but he has always had an appetite for learning and is always seeking more knowledge.

Beautiful Moments is an insightful poem by David which is a small token of how he views life.

BEAUTIFUL MOMENTS

When the sun comes up and the birds begin to sing,
When the grass is cut, and the fresh smell it brings,
These are beautiful moments to cherish and enjoy,
Or when a child unwraps his Christmas presents, to find their favourite toy.

I love how a carpet forms when a tree sheds its autumn leaves,
I love the spring and the blossom it brings,
I like to keep warm in winter, but I like to watch the children play in the snow,
But summer is my favourite season, when fragrant flowers begin to grow.

I love the sound of church bells, especially on wedding days,
I enjoy the sound of the ocean, and rolling of the waves,

I love to hear a bee humming, as it pollinates a flower,
I enjoy the ticking of the clock as it strikes the midnight hour.

BEAUTIFUL MOMENTS

Beautiful moments are there for all to hear, smell and see,
However, yours may be very different, as mine are to me,
But life is full of beauty, and many wondrous things,
Like migrating birds, for they too have their songs to sing.

"Belief in success is the one basic, absolutely essential ingredient of successful people."

— David J. Schwartz

The Magic of Thinking Big

The magic of thinking big has been a concept that many have embraced recently, however this concept has not been easy to implement successfully unless you have a great guru to follow. Over the years I have been rather fascinated by the concept of thinking big and through all my research I have found many interesting facts, speculations and revelations of which some I hope to share with you in this book.

When I think of the concept which is the magic of thinking big, I need to refer you to the two good books which have really enlightened me; although I am sure there are many of them on this subject as I have seen so many already. However, as a starting point, I would with confidence refer you to start with these two books; I believe that they will give you are a good starting insight on the concept of the magic of thinking big.

The Magic of Thinking Big

The first book which I was very fond of reading is called Bring Out the Magic in Your Mind by Al Koran. This book explains the concept in a simple and implementable manner. When it was first published in 1965 it was a best seller and for good reason. Al Koran was a British mentalist, author and inventor, before becoming the now famous magician who went on to lecture at Cambridge University and immigrated to the USA in 1969. Al Koran died in 1972.

One of the things that Al Koran was most aware of was that all magicians must have belief. Belief is the most important thing for anyone who wants to work with magic. The subconscious mind is the part of the mind which regulates the heart, breathing and digestive system. The conscious mind is the mind we use every day and which we use to think and speak. It is the subconscious mind which brings out the magic. It never sleeps and it keeps a record of every moment; everything you have said, felt and done in your life.

No one really knows the limits of its powers. At the age of seven it was apparent that Al Koran, whose real name was Edward Doe, had a natural talent and was gifted with a sixth sense and extrasensory perception, which grew well into his adult life.

Change Your Words Change Your Life

This led him to gain the title of the world's greatest mind reader and the greatest magician in the world.

He became so popular that he would receive letters, phone calls and telegrams from all over the world. It was essential for him to maintain a private life as so many people wanted to win prizes and make money using his intuition. It was for this reason that his home address was a secret and not even his friends knew where he lived.

He had a great respect for his powers and would only use them for good. The reason why he wrote his book was to advise people on how to obtain what they desired through the power of belief. He did a lot of research and attended many different meetings which included the scientific, occult and all others of a spiritual nature.

He researched the minds of men and woman through history, and met many personalities that had reached the top of their professions. All his research led him to believe this one amazing discovery; that the power of belief can lead you to health, wealth, love and prosperity.

In other words, to achieve what you want in life, the first thing you need is to believe. It is the in word belief or knowing that brings outword results. Why not start your day saying I believe; I Believe; I believe.

There are so many stories about the power of belief that it would probably fill the Encyclopedia-Britannica, but perhaps the majority of individuals remain skeptical? It is a big irony that some of the most intelligent people in life are relatively poor, and that some people with little or no education become wealthy.

Why is this do you think?

There is power in knowledge, but only when you are ready to accept it. Visualization is a key factor in achieving your dreams and desires. In order to achieve what you want you need to have a clear vision in order for it to come to fruition. You need to be super optimistic and practice visualization daily. Do your visualization every night before you go to bed. It is vital that your visualisation is documented daily.

There can be no doubts whatsoever; you must believe it to achieve it. You must see in your mind exactly what you want. Develop a feeling of expectancy. Having said that, you must accept what you already have with gratitude, for with gratitude you have the power to create great magic and achieve all that you desire.

Change Your Words Change Your Life

When you live a life full of gratitude, you are allowing your subconscious to operate at a higher level, which allows magic to take place and allows your desires to be fulfilled.

If you get rid of ingratitude and resentment then this will allow the magic to flow. You can go through life moaning and groaning or you can be grateful. The choice is yours. I think you already know which set of attitudes would bring the best results.

Stand in front of the mirror and tell yourself that your life is filled with health, wealth and happiness and believe it. Say it with passion and emotion in order to achieve your goals and it is essential to visualize them. When you become more relaxed, focus on your dreams instead of focusing on negative thoughts, you are opening the way for the subconscious to work more effectively.

It is essential to get rid of being ungrateful, resentful and grumpy, as this will block your way to getting what you desire. A magician says abracadabra before performing his tricks as it means speak the blessing. To work magic in your life and achieve your dreams you need to bless what you already have as this will bring to you a more satisfying life.

I can see lots of people enjoying reading this book and lots of people buying it and wanting to read it. Yes, visualization is a key factor in helping you achieve your dreams.

The second book I would like to recommend is a book written by David J. Schwartz titled The Magic of Thinking Big which was published back in 1959 and by 2015 over six million copies had been sold and it is still being sold today. David was a professor at Georgia State University and was considered to be a leading authority on motivation.

He was very well known through his self-help books and through his publications. His book The Magic of Thinking Big is an excellent guide on how to make your dreams come true by thinking positively and by changing your habits as well to positive ones.

Visualisation is a key component of his strategy along with goal setting. He explains that there are three main reasons for failure; excusitis procrastination and detail.

The are many books written about how to improve your lot in life and with films like The Secret, which was watched by millions, it would be interesting to see how many people actually achieved their goals and dreams.

I suspect it would not be many in the scheme of things. I think one of the main reasons for this is

Change Your Words Change Your Life

because the subconscious mind needs to be repeatedly told what your goals and dreams are and it needs time to process new information.

Visualization always plays its part and the emotional feeling has to be strong. Perseverance and persistence are the keys to achieving your dreams and it is undoubtable that it is prudent to practice being perseverant and persistent daily. Another issue of course is it is often friends and family who should support you who sometimes discourage rather than help. And in these circumstances the lack of believing will cause the magic to soon disappear.

In order to achieve success in any area in life, it often calls for stepping out of your comfort zone and a substantial number of people have difficulty overcoming this issue. Procrastination and fear often prevent people from taking up new challenges.

In order to overcome these problems, a best-selling book was written by Susan Jeffers called Feel the Fear and Do It anyway.

This book offers insight on how to deal with these problems.

Apart from reading books and following what others are teaching it is also good to find things that make sense to you throughout life. Look at every new thing in life as something which can contribute to the big thinking mindset.

For instance, take the example of a well-known grocery chain in the UK which uses a phrase in their advertising which I found can be readily applied in our everyday lives as it complements the big thinking mindset. The slogan refers to time and says "when it's gone it's gone". This is so true because in the scheme of things a man's time on earth is over in the blink of an eye.

Always being on time for appointments and accepting how important it is to make each moment count is vital to your every day. I believe that Robert De Niro said it best when he said, *"Time goes on, whatever you are going to do, do it now don't wait."* And I agree with this 100%, just think of it, if you have to spend your life waiting for the perfect timing to do anything, you will never get anything done.

Tomorrow is never guaranteed and yes; we should plan for it. But without living as well as you can today; how can you know if you will be able to try it tomorrow?

Some people want to wait for the perfect moment to begin and to wait for everything to be favourable before starting anything, be it a new job, their own business, becoming an author, following their dreams, even having children or getting married; and yes, there are times when plans really should be better scheduled. However, it's the desire for perfection, and yes perfection is very desirable, which tends to delay your start and by the time your perfect time arrives it could be too late.

So be mindful and pick your tasks for today, think big and get them done. Yet, also keep in mind that sometimes it is good to take a step back and pause to observe and then continue on with your journey.

I recently wrote a poem called 'Pause' which can be worth reflecting upon.

Pause

Pause to watch the raindrops running down the pane.
Pause to watch a child splashing in the rain.
Pause to think of all the good we can still do.
Pause to think more positive thoughts and make all your dreams come true.

Pause to listen to the birds singing their early morning song.
Pause to be grateful, happy as each day comes along.

The Magic of Thinking Big

Pause to feel your heartbeat, and pause your body too.
Pause to look at the good in all that you do.

Pause to take a breath of fresh air,
Pause to know that there are people who care. Pause to pray that the world becomes a safer place. Pause to send love to each and every race.

I also think that from the musical South Pacific a quote worth mentioning is; "You got to have a dream, if you don't have a dream how is it supposed to come true." This rings true because when you think of it, a farmer will never have crops to plough if he did not sow the seeds first.

Which leads me to a particular seed of thought which really inspired me, the words filled my mind with a realization as I had listened to what was considered to be the greatest speeches by Winston Churchill and which had gone on to become the most famous phrase, which is, *"Never give up, never give up, never give up."*

The simple take away from the concept of thinking big is dream big and if you believe in your dreams you can achieve them. Sometimes setbacks are just a stepping stone from which we can learn and once

Change Your Words Change Your Life

we start learning from our mistakes and setbacks, we know we are learning, because we know we can turn a losing situation into a winning one.

This concept has become such a powerful one that so many successful people in the world have had great inspirational lines which you can use to keep inspired when things get tough. Inspirational quotes which have helped me over the years.

> *"All dreams can come true if we have the courage to pursue them."*
>
> **— Walt Disney**

> *"Develop an attitude of gratitude and give thanks for everything that happens to you, knowing that every step forward is a step toward achieving something bigger and better than your current situation."*
>
> **— Brian Tracy**

> *"You are what you think. So just think big, believe big, act big, work big, give big, forgive big, laugh big, love big and live big."*
>
> **— Andrew Carnegie**

The Magic of Thinking Big

> *"Create the highest, grandest vision possible for your life, because you become what you believe."*
>
> **—Oprah Winfrey**

> *"Let me tell you something you already know. The world ain't all sunshine and rainbows. It's a very mean and nasty place, and I don't care how tough you are, it will beat you to your knees and keep you there permanently if you let it. You, me, or nobody is gonna hit as hard as life. But it ain't about how hard you hit. It's about how hard you can get hit and keep moving forward; how much you can take and keep moving forward.*
>
> *That's how winning is done! Now, if you know what you're worth, then go out and get what you're worth. But you gotta be willing to take the hits, and not pointing fingers saying you ain't where you wanna be because of him, or her, or anybody. Cowards do that and that ain't you. You're better than that! I'm always gonna love you, no matter what. No matter what happens. You're my son and you're my blood. You're the best thing in my life. But until you start believing in yourself, you ain't gonna have a life."*
>
> **—Sylvester Stallone in the film Rocky**

Change Your Words Change Your Life

I hope that these famous quotes which have helped so many will help you keep inspired and that the two books on thinking big will clarify the concept for you as they have done for me. I have found that the concept of the magic of thinking big is one that everyone should try as it is an addiction worth getting hooked on.

We will now break it down further as we dive into the individual aspects which each play a role in the concept of thinking big starting with a preparation segment on the power of words and how you will be using your words throughout your magic journey to help you grow.

THE HEART OF THE MATTER

Take down the wall you have built around your heart, Throw the baggage away and make a new start,
Dreams come true if you believe in yourself,
By taking positive action you can improve your wealth.
All the answers can be found within,
Listen to your heart, and you will eventually win, A life that is happy as you want it to be,
Just think and focus on the changes you want to see.

31

The Magic of Thinking Big

Be grateful to your heart, because it knows what you need,
Be digging the garden, you can remove the weeds,
Happy thoughts will grow like flowers you adore, To a life of abundance, joy and wonders never cease,
And when your prayers are answered, you will then know peace.

The Power of the Written and Spoken Word

Words are more powerful than many people realise, especially those you say to yourself; they have a far greater impact than you could ever imagine. It is vital that the words you use, especially when talking to yourself are positive, and uplifting. In order to increase the power of positive words, a well-known technique is talking to yourself in front of the mirror.

It does make a difference when you tell yourself that you are doing OK, and that you are doing better and that you are getting success every day of your life. It is most important that when you say the words out loud, that look at your face and see the words come back to you.

Throughout the book you will be using your words along with inspirational quotes to help you develop yourself on your journey of embracing the concept of the magic of thinking big.

The Power of the Written and Spoken Word

A book which really illustrated the power of words is called The Secret of Perfect Living by James T Mangan, who lived between 1896 and1970. James was an author, a visionary, an excellent speech writer and a family man who even found time to compete as a top spinner and was champion at one point too. I recommend that you invest in his book because it has been most valuable to me to discover the power of using certain words in certain circumstances.

After he had completed thousands of studies and almost 45 years of research, I would highly recommend this book. He started his research into words with the book called Switch Words. With the use of Switch Words you can:

1. Conquer all fears,
2. Learn to relax,
3. Overcome despair and blue moods.
4. Keep yourself forever young.
5. Get along better with other people.
6. Set goals and achieve them.
7. Gain money and prosperity
8. Free yourself of bad habits.
9. Begin to know yourself.
10. Begin to release your abilities.
11. Be a permanently happy person and deal with setbacks more effectively.

Change Your Words Change Your Life

Activity 1

Let's start you off with a simple one-line affirmation which will inspire you for the day. Remember what you will be saying to yourself must be inspirational, positive, and uplifting. You must really see yourself when you say the words, and take yourself seriously too.

Below I have examples which you need to adjust or change to fit you.

I am Beautiful…
I am Loving…
I am Kind…
I am Honest…
I am Reliable…
I am trustworthy…
I am genuine…
I am fun…
I am a good friend…
I am a good sibling…
I am a good parent / child…
I am a good person…

The Power of the Written and Spoken Word

Pick your own words and say them out loud every day until you begin to rewire the way that you think. You can also look for inspiring quotes from great leaders and speakers, and draw from their words to gain more inspiration and confidence in all that you do. I have added many of the quotes which have helped me so that you have a starting point.

One of my Favourite quotes by Benjamin Franklin which has helped me a lot through life is, *"From the seed of adversity comes the seed of an even greater benefit."*

So, keep in mind that if you think negative thoughts you will attract negative things into your life. If you think of positive you will attract more positive in your life.

You can see how important it is to think and be in a positive frame of mind, most if not all of the time. You can only do this by focusing on all the good things that have happened in your life. By being grateful for everything that happens in your day, no matter how small, but we will get to how you can do that a little later.

I write poems about being positive, and I know that they inspire people, and if they are shared or help just one person then they have been worthwhile writing.

Change Your Words Change Your Life

One poem I wrote is a poem called 'Words'; I hope it helps to inspire you.

Words

Some are beautiful, some are sad
Some words are good and others are bad.
But the only words that count are the words you think If you focus on negative words you will only sink.

Positive and creative words are the only words you need
Plant them in your mind and they will grow like seed
Onto blossom and flowers to brighten your day
They will only make you feel better in every way.

So just dust down your thoughts and take out the weeds.
Just plant positive thoughts and plant positive seeds
By thinking on the bright side in all that you do.
You will have more sunshine in your life and be happier too.

The Power of the Written and Spoken Word

"Belief in success is the one basic, absolutely essential ingredient of successful people."

— **David J. Schwartz**

'Miracles happen to those who believe in them.'

— **Bernard Berenson**

The Power of Belief

Harnessing the power of belief can profoundly change your life; you can reinvent yourself and achieve and become anything you want in life. Two famous quotes which I found describe the power of belief perfectly

"Whatever the mind can conceive and believe, it can achieve,"

—Napoleon Hill

"The mind is everything. What you think, you become,"

—Buddha.

You can choose what you want to believe, but the main problem is that during the first seven years of your life, your thought patterns are created and formed. If you were brought up in a supportive and motivational environment, it will be a great help later in life should you face addictive issues.

However, if you were brought up in a difficult environment you will carry these experiences into

The Power of Belief

your adult life without realising it. The key to changing your life comes within. In you are having issue in your life, listen to your inner voice and you will receive guidance.

Don't be too hard on yourself or use negative words to beat yourself up. In order to develop an unshakeable belief in yourself you will need to have a positive circle of friends who will help build you up in life, you don't need negative people in your life as they will bring you down.

So, if any of your friends are particularly negative, I would suggest you let them go as life is too short to be advised by negative thinkers. We all have the power to choose our thoughts, choose them wisely, believe in yourself, think positive and read all these inspiring books or listen to the recordings.

Think success, don't think of failure. There are many things you can do to change the way you think and believe in yourself. There are many subliminal audios on how to uplift the way of your thinking. One of the world's leading authorities, Morry Zelcovitch can help you change your thought patterns, or you can get help from one of the world's many leading motivational speakers

who have helped millions of people to improve their thinking. You can find many options on YouTube and

Change Your Words Change Your Life

I know that they will help you as they have helped me and so many others already.

A few quotes to inspire you to believe in yourself and guide you on your path to success are:

"You can get anything in life that you want if you help enough people to get what they want."

— **Zig Ziglar**

"You don't have to be great at something to start but you have to start to be great at something."

— **Zig Ziglar**

Activity 2

To get you started on your journey to believe in yourself I have set out a repetitive task for you for the next two weeks.

Remember to continue with activity 1 from the previous chapter.

The Power of Belief

Monday

Write down your hopes and dreams for the future and how you believe you can achieve them by answering the following questions.

1.   Do you already believe in yourself, rate your level of self-belief out of 10?

_____

2.   What is it that you wish to achieve in your personal life?

_____

3.   What is it that you wish to achieve in your professional life?

_____

4.   What obstacle do you think is standing in the way of you believing in yourself?

_____

_____

5. Is there a solution to getting over the obstacle that is preventing you from believing in yourself?

_____

6. Would you need, help getting over the obstacle?

_____

7. Do you know anyone who can help you get over the obstacle?

_____

8. What have you noticed while completing this exercise?

_____

_____

_____

The Power of Belief

Tuesday – Saturday (Repeat)

1. Stand in front of the mirror and repeat this chant three times before starting your day – "I have big dreams. I believe I can achieve my dreams by believing in myself"

2. How did you feel while and after telling yourself that you believe in you?

_____

3. Did you believe what you said?

_____

4. How did it affect your day?

_____

_____

_____

_____

Change Your Words Change Your Life

Sunday

1. Stand in front of the mirror and repeat this chant three times before starting your day – "I have big dreams. I believe I can achieve my dreams by believing in myself"

2. How did you feel while and after telling yourself that you believe in you?

   _____

3. Did you believe what you said?

   _____

4. How did it affect your day?

   _____

5. How much more did you believe yourself today? Rate your self-belief out of 10.

_____

6. What difference do you see in your belief rating between Monday and Sunday?

_____

'Repeat for at least another week.

After the end of the exercise on Sunday the 14th day review how you have gone on, and give yourself a rating on your belief level.

If the rating has not improved, continue with the practice until your confidence level has increased to a more acceptable level.

"As we express our gratitude, we must never forget that the highest appreciation is not to utter words, but to live by them."

—John F. Kennedy

The Power of Gratitude

It is only when you begin to study the benefits of being grateful is it when you discover the importance of Gratitude in your life. And the more I looked at the power of gratitude the more I realised how being grateful can have a long-lasting effect on your life.

Gratitude can help you sleep better, it can improve your physical being, it will open doors to new relationships and it will also improve your mental health. People really appreciate being thanked.

One of the ways of increasing the gratitude in your life is to start a gratitude diary listing all the things you are grateful for. This can then be used to focus on all the positive things in your life. Keeping a gratitude journal can definitely change your life; I know it has changed mine. It will make you focus on all the positive things in your life and help you become more positive overall.

It will need to be a consistent activity which you do routinely on a daily basis and you should include anything you are grateful for. It's prudent to include in the book anything and everything no matter how insignificant it may seem to be.

Becoming a volunteer can also help you become more grateful, because while you are helping others you tend to realise how much you actually have to be grateful for; rather than sitting nitpicking at your own issues and problems.

Also, spending time with the people you love will help you be more grateful as love is the ultimate emotion to boost gratitude and it will help you express more happiness in your life. Spending time with loved ones is also prudent because each passing moment might be our last, tomorrow is not guaranteed and today will be over in a blink of an eye. So, make the most of every moment and be grateful to have it.

Never miss an opportunity to tell someone you love them and how much you appreciate them, you never know how much those kind words might make a difference in their day or ultimately in their lives. Notice the beauty of nature, smile more often and watch inspirational videos to remind yourself of all the good in the world which is often overlooked in a time of adversity. I have written a few poems on the power of gratitude and I have included them below as I hope they can be of some benefit.

Change Your Words Change Your Life

The Magic of Gratitude

Gratitude dissolves negativity, try it is true
It sweeps the cobwebs and stops you feeling blue.
Being grateful is a wonderful state of mind
It will bring more happiness and peace of every kind.

Always look for the good and that is what you will find.
While gratitude can bring you more love and peace of mind
It is a word that can bring you magic and success By being grateful you can achieve your best

Gratitude, replaces fear with love Like a gift from heaven above
Always be grateful even when times are bleak For this can attract all the happiness you seek.

I am Grateful

Being more grateful now, is what I need to be Then I believe the universe will open up to me.
An attitude of gratitude needs to be a passion for me And with enough practise, like driving a car will develop automatically.
I need to be grateful for being alive and well.
I want gratitude to be ingrained in my life, and part of every cell.
I appreciate everything I have in my life and even look for the good in all my strife.
For I can only grow when I focus on where I want to be
And this will reduce my stress and combat my negativity.

I am grateful for all the beautiful people in my life and family.
I am grateful for all the help I receive from technology.

I am grateful to recognize now how important gratitude is to me
The world needs more gratitude to bring peace and harmony.

THE MOON AND THE STARS

Would you like to dance under the moon and the stars? Life is not all about jewels and cars.
Loving each day, and being grateful for what you have got,
It's just a starting point, but it means a lot.

Stars twinkle and the moon can shine, Laughter and joy can be divine,
But loving yourself comes high on the list,
Be true to yourself and emerge from the mist.

The moon and the stars never go away, but we only pass just once this way, Never forget that love is the key,
It's mankind's answer to you and me.

REMEMBER

Remember there is beauty in the silence, if you listen to the sound,
Remember when life gets hard, it can be turned around,
Remember to be grateful when the sun comes up each day,

Remember to count your blessings, when you sit down and pray.

Remember not to be too serious, for we are all just passing through,
Remember that life is full of mystery, but we can all learn something new,
Remember when the day is done, and we go to bed at night,
Remember to look forward to another day, when we see the morning light.

Change Your Words Change Your Life

Remember that nothing can be taken for granted, but we can only do our best,
Remember to love yourself, to work, play and rest,
Remember that laughter helps us to be happy, and reduces our stress,
Remember that all our answers can come from within, because they do know you best.

A JOURNAL OF GRATITUDE.

No more pity parties, no more woe is me,
You have to clear negativity, in order to be free, Look for the bright side, in everything you do,

You have to be positive, to make your dreams come true.
In order to be joyful, loving and kind,
You need to banish negativity, right out of your mind,
By focusing on your joy, your vibrational level will increase,

Your life will be happier, and you will find peace.

The Power of Gratitude

What you think about expands, believe me it's true,
So try to be positive, in all that you do,
Be more grateful, and record your gratitude each day,
And you will find an amazing inner peace will come your way.

Activity 3

Gratitude is the fastest way to get yourself to a happy place while attracting more abundance and positivity to you.

Every night before your go to bed take a moment to write five new things that you have to be grateful for. Each new thing needs to be entirely new and not have been included in your diary before.

Write these out in a form of a gratitude statement such as…

I am so grateful that I have a wonderful job.

I am so grateful for my best friend because she always makes me laugh.

I am grateful for the amazing lunch I had today.

Change Your Words Change Your Life

I am grateful for the strawberries and cream I had this evening; they were delicious.

To get you started with this activity I have a few additional questions which you can fill in below for the next two weeks so that you can get in the habit of journaling your gratitude.

Remember to continue with activities 1 and 2 from the previous chapter.

Combined activity

1.   How has it changed your approach from day to day with implementing both Gratitude and Belief?

_____

2.   Have you still been consistent with the daily activities?

_____

3. Has it become easier to both believe in yourself and be grateful?

_____

"We ask ourselves, 'Who am I to be brilliant, gorgeous, talented, fabulous?' Actually, who are you not to be? You are a child of God. Your playing small does not serve the world. There is nothing enlightened about shrinking so that other people won't feel insecure around you.

We are all meant to shine, as children do. We were born to make manifest the glory of God that is within us. It's not just in some of us; it's in everyone. And as we let our own light shine, we unconsciously give other people permission to do the same. As we are liberated from our own fear, our presence automatically liberates others."

— Marianne Williamson,

A Return to Love:
Reflections on the Principles of
A Course in Miracles

The Importance of Self-esteem

In October 2019 I went with my special friend to a two day a seminar in London to listen to Marisa Peer who is a world-renowned speaker; she is a (RTT) Rapid Transformational Therapy Trainer and bestselling author. She has over three decades of experience in hypnotherapy and has treated millions of people. One of the things she said was how powerful words are and I knew that before I went to see her. But after listening to her over two days, I realised I had really underestimated how powerful words are.

She said that one of the main issues that people have today is low self-esteem. I've been interested in Marisa's work for years now and when I had the opportunity to go to her seminar I knew I wanted to go. She wrote the book called I Am Enough; and I knew I wanted to read it. In this inspirational book she indicated that the three words, "I am enough" can change your life and can certainly boost your self-esteem.

The Importance of Self-esteem

I recommend that anyone who has self-esteem issues read her book. The book is designed to increase your own sense of self-worth and to make you feel good about yourself.

The book inspired me to write a poem called 'I am enough'. I hope this helps to inspire you.

I am enough

I'm enough and so are you
Be true to yourself in all that you do. Look in the mirror and see yourself smile Be confident and happy
Then you can go the extra mile.

A key to life is to love yourself more
Praise yourself daily and your self-esteem will soar.
Live in the moment and improve what you can do
Learn to accept what you can't change and be grateful too.

Have a strong sense of purpose but be helpful and kind.

Change Your Words Change Your Life

Focus on your good points to help rewire your mind Be responsible and loving in all that you do I am enough and so are you.

There are several things that you can do to improve your self-esteem, but the best way to start would be to start with the easy things like:

Be nice to yourself, YES... I said it. Cut yourself some slack every once in a while, and every day compliment yourself. You will be amazed how it will change how you see yourself when you start being your own friend rather than your own judge.

I have a little exercise for you to repeat over the next two weeks. Once you have done it fill in how it made you feel in the spaces left for you on each day's page.

Monday – Saturday (Repeat)

Stand in front of the mirror, and say one complimentary thing about yourself, it needs to be something good, positive and kind.

The Importance of Self-esteem

1. How hard was it to compliment yourself?

   _____

2. How did the compliment make you feel?

   _____

Sunday

Stand in front of the mirror, and say one complimentary thing about yourself, it needs to be something good, positive and kind.

1. How hard was it to compliment yourself?

   _____

2. How did the compliment make you feel?

   _____

3.   How much has changed about yourself esteem since Monday?

_____

Combined activity

1.   How has it changed your approach from day to day with implementing both Gratitude and Belief?

_____

2.   Have you still been consistent with the daily activities?

_____

3.   Has it become easier to believe in yourself and be grateful now that you have been less judgmental of yourself?

_____

The Importance of Self-esteem

Now that you have learned to believe in yourself, be grateful and be your own friend; you are well on your way to start finding self-love. Yes, it sounds all sorts of wrong, but I assure you that it is all sorts of right, trust me.

You need to love yourself whenever you can. Focus on what you love and what makes you happy, and remember that no one is perfect and everyone makes mistakes.

Try not to get hung up on things that you can't control and be happy instead of focusing on what didn't go well. Louise Hay who sold millions of books during her lifetime, and was a motivational speaker across the world said it best when she said: *"Remember, you have been criticizing yourself for years and it hasn't worked. Try approving of yourself and see what happens."*

It's not easy to love yourself when the world around you is so judgmental and society teaches us to self-judge on a daily basis. But we need to stand strong for ourselves, only then can we make our dreams come true, only then can we embrace love from or give love to others.

Below I have a few quotes from well-known icons around the world to help you keep inspired to love yourself.

Change Your Words Change Your Life

"Love yourself first and everything else falls in line, you really have to love yourself to get anything done in this world."

— Lucille Ball

"What lies behind us and what lies before us are tiny matters compared to what lies within us."

— Ralph Waldo Emerson

"To establish true self-esteem we must focus on our successes and forget about the failures and the negatives in our lives."

— Denis Waitley

These are only a few great lines to help you, and if you are looking for more, there are amazing and free self-love inspirational content pieces all over social media and especially on YouTube.

Self-Confidence

Without sufficient self-confidence you are most likely to struggle with several aspects of your life, both professionally and personally as in your work environment self-confidence is what makes you stand

The Importance of Self-esteem

out. It is what lets you take risks and offer your assistance. In your personal life, self-confidence will affect how others see you, approach you and interact with you, which determine how the relationships in your life will be as well. So, in order to become successful, you need to do some work on yourself.

There are many ways of increasing your self-confidence yet they all start with improving your self-belief and your self-gratitude, as well as your self-esteem.

There are many great speakers who you can listen to on YouTube to help you build your self- confidence; however, you can start by thinking how your self-confidence has already improved since the start of the activities in the Power of Belief chapter.

You can also dive deeper into expanding your control of your self-confidence by making use of hypno-therapists. One of my favourite hypnotists who has an outstanding programme for dealing with self-confidence is a neuro-linguistic programmer by the name of Jim Katsoulis.

He has helped over 3000 clients and he has helped change many people's lives. You can use self-hypnosis to reprogramme your mind and for self-confidence. He has a programme known as the 30 minute program which will help condition your

Change Your Words Change Your Life

mind. I have this programme myself and it certainly works.

Note: I am not gaining any financial gain for recommending this program but I do know that it works.

The truth of the matter is that you have to be careful of the thoughts that you think. By thinking negative thoughts you will bring down your life, but by changing your thoughts you can change your life.

I wrote a poem about changing your thoughts which I have included, I hope you enjoy it.

Changing Your Thoughts

Life can be easy, life can be tough Life can be smooth, life can be rough Life can be happy, life can be sad Life can be good, life can be bad

What you focus on is what you get
Focus on happiness and your needs will be met.
Think happiness, feel happiness, see happiness, talk happiness and it will come to pass.

The Importance of Self-esteem

Focus on happiness and it will last.

So, by changing your thoughts you can change your life

By focusing on happiness, you can turn darkness to light.

Words are so powerful so be careful what you think and say.

Believe in yourself and life will be better in every way. Decide to be happy and grateful too.

Gratitude and happiness can make your dreams come true.

WHO'S PERFECT ANYWAY

I don't have to be perfect, I just have to be me,
Sometimes I am as daft as a brush, my silliness is there for all to see,
But life should be full of laughter and full of joy,
I've always looked at life differently, even when I was a boy.

Happiness at the end of the day, is what we all seek,
But sometimes life isn't perfect and goes up the creek,
When that happens, I try to think of all the good things that have happened to me,
Negative thoughts can bring you down, but gratitude will set you free.

"Look for the good," is what I say,
If you look hard enough, you will find it in every day,
Because what you focus on is what you get,
By focusing on good things, your needs will be met.

Activity 4

There are several other simple ways that you can build up your self-confidence and you should try these along with the activities 1 – 3 from the previous chapters.

1. Adjusting your posture, by slouching your posture shows you lack self-confidence as it hides you from the world. Try for the next two weeks to

The Importance of Self-esteem

consciously adjust your posture and make a conscious decision to stand or sit up straight.

2. Eating healthily; how many times have you heard you are what you eat? Well, the fact of the matter is that some foods are filled with nutrients which either boost the endorphins for happiness, or the endorphins for depression. Make a point of it to eat one fruit per day which has a high level of nutrients which make you feel better.

3. Smile more, yes it's hard when you are sad or angry; to be smiling instead of crying or screaming is a conscious decision you have to make which overrides the subconscious reaction to the unfavourable emotion. By overriding your body's reaction, you can gradually override your emotion as well. So, make a point of it to smile at least 10 times every day.

4. Find new affirmations to boost your self-confidence until you find one that works for you.

One of the affirmations which I enjoyed is:

"Every day, in every way, I am getting better and better."

— Émile Coué

Change Your Words Change Your Life

John Lennon wrote a pop song in 1980 called 'Beautiful Boy' where he used Émile Coué's affirmation in the lyrics.

5. You should also create your own affirmations, things that you can say to yourself which are more relevant and befitting to your needs.

a. Along with your activities from the previous chapters add on a daily affirmation to build your self-confidence.

Below are a few samples to start off with: I am solution orientated,

All problems are solvable

I am a success magnet,

I attract success in everything I do I have greatness within me

I am good and honest.

I deserve to be successful.

The Value of Forgiveness

Developing the ability to forgive will help you decrease stress and will help you release anxiety and stress as well as unnecessary anger within your life. Forgiveness not only frees the mind of cluttered frustration and thermal but it also frees your body from the tense reactions to every dark thought which the lack of forgiveness causes.

Alexander Pope recognised the value of forgiveness when he wrote, 'to err is human, to forgive divine'. When someone hurts you with their words, it can lead to anger, bitterness and even vengeance. However, if we decide not to forgive, you might be the one that pays the price.

Forgiveness doesn't mean forgetting, or excusing the behaviour or action, but the benefits gained from forgiveness can lead to peace of mind for the person who forgives. It will also lead to better relationships, better health as wells as a stronger immune system and a stronger heart. Writing in a journal, praying and using meditation can help with the process of forgiveness.

The Value of Forgiveness

A famous quote which helped me understand the concept of setting yourself free by forgiving others is the quote by Lewis B. Smedes *"To forgive is to set a prisoner free and discover that the prisoner was you."* This really got me thinking; take a moment to think of it too. When you get upset or depressed or hold onto the things that bring bad emotions into your world, not only do you suffer by mentally being run down or worn out, but also your body starts to take a toll because of the stress that those emotions bring into your life.

Thus, it traps you in a cycle of struggle where the pain, anger and physical symptoms become your prison. But with forgiving you set yourself free of all that.

Although what was done to you stays with you and still leaves its mark, it no longer weights you down, it no longer exhausts your body and mind. It's as simple as understanding the meaning of the quote by Catherine Ponder an American minister who has written over a dozen books including several best sellers, *"When you hold resentment toward another, you are bound to that person or condition by an emotional link that is stronger than steel. Forgiveness is the only way to dissolve that link and get free."*

You might also know of the famous quote, *"To forgive is the highest, most beautiful form of love. In return, you will receive untold peace and happiness."* — **Robert Muller**

Marion Williamson an American author who has written several bestselling books said, "The practice of forgiveness is our most important contribution to healing the world." Do I forgive, I certainly do my best to forgive as much as I can, but I do not forget.

I wrote a poem some time ago about Forgiveness and it's called benefiting from forgiveness and I hope that it will help inspire you.

Benefiting from Forgiveness

When you learn to forgive it sets you free You develop more clarity and energy
It will help grumpiness, sourness and depression disappear.
Friendships will improve and solutions will appear.

It will free up your mental and emotional state.

The Value of Forgiveness

It will give you more happiness and put a smile on your face.

You should see you friends and have more peace of mind.

You will have a feeling of lightness and become more loving and kind.

It will release stuck anger, resentment and pain You have nothing to lose and everything to gain.

You will become stronger and more positive day by day.

Your unhappy thoughts will just float away.

Activity 5

Forgiving is not easy along with your daily tasks from the previous activities 1-4 , work of forgiving both yourself and others.

Each day remind yourself earnestly by saying to yourself daily

Change Your Words Change Your Life

1   Today I forgive myself for . . .

(List a different thing every day)

_____

_____

2.   I forgive . . .

(The name of someone who has wronged you) For (what they did).

_____

_____

Keep doing this daily along with your new daily activities from the previous chapters.

Vibrational Levels

Dr DAVID R. HAWKINS' MAP OF CONSIOUSNESS SCALE shows us the best representation of the vibrational levels and his scale is an internationally recognised system.

It goes without saying that it is because David R. Hawkins, is an MD with a Phd. and because his work is proven to the extent where he has been knighted and honoured worldwide with titles he authored such as *"Foremost Teacher of Enlightenment"* and *"Bodhisativa"*, Dr. Hawkins is a widely known authority within the fields of consciousness research and spirituality, he has written and taught from the unique perspective of an experienced clinician, scientist, and mystic. His life was devoted to the spiritual evolution of mankind.

I have set out below all the qualities included in this list

Enlightenment – 700 – 1000

Peace – 600

Love – 500

Vibrational Levels

Reason – 400

Acceptance – 350

Willingness – 310

Neutrality – 250

Courage – 200

Pride – 175

Anger – 150

Desire – 125

Fear – 100

Grief – 75

Empathy – 50

Guilt – 30

Shame – 20.

There are a number of ways you can raise the level of your vibrations and one of the ways is by changing your thoughts. You need to focus your mind on positive thoughts especially when negative thinking starts to become a pattern of your regular thought pattern.

Change Your Words Change Your Life

It is recommended that you drink plenty of water, and be aware of all the foods you eat. Even if you meditate 10 min per day this can help you be more peaceful and can help release the stress that has built up over the day.

Your vibration state requires movement and by being active your vibrational levels will increase. Exercise, dance and Tai Chi for example will help reduce stress and anxiety.

Christie Marie Sheldon is one of the world's leading energy leaders and her goal is to help a million people achieve their potential. Her work on vibrational levels is worth looking into if you want to find more information on this subject.

At the end of the day whatever techniques you try, it is something you have to continue for it to work, hopefully I have given you some to help you find success and happiness.

A Note on Self-development Experts

By far and away, the self-improvement and self-development field is dominated by America and is a billion dollar industry however Japan has its own share of self-development experts. One of the reasons for the amazing growth in the Japanese economy over many years is the system they use called kaizen.

There are a number of books written on the subject but basically it is a Japanese management philosophy which helps to improve productivity in an organisation by taking a number of small but simple steps that leads to an overall improvement.

The improvement works on the principal working from the bottom up, where people work to improve their methods on a combined and continual basis. These small continued improvements over time can result in a major improvement. Kaizen is the Japanese word meaning improvement; it is pronounced 'Kai' which means continues and 'Zen' which means improvement.

A Note on Self-development Experts

Over many years I have been involved with looking at ways to improve myself and one company, that I have had many courses with is Mindvalley, the founder Vishen Lakhiani has built up a world class organisation which offers many programmes for self-improvement and development and I recommend that you have a look as they offer some free programmes and free seminars too.

Their aim is to give you the opportunity to reach your fullest potential of your mind body and spirit. On YouTube Mindvalley advertises extensively and recently they gave a talk with Ken Honda who has sold over seven million copies of his books which include works that can be categorised between finance and personal development field, with special attention on personal wealth and happiness through self-analysis.

It is Ken Honda's mission to make the world a better place to live and he has interviewed many of the top money handlers in Japan and from one of his interviews he had revealed a secret from a billionaire. He said, *"you should arigato your money."*

Every time you spend money or receive money you should say the word arigato, this means thank you in Japanese. The concept is *"The more you appreciate money, the more money will appreciate you."*

A Few More Poems to Keep you Inspired

BE HAPPY NOW

The past has gone, You cannot change it.

The future has not arrived, only now exists. Our ultimate aim is to be happy,
Choose to feel good now. Happiness attracts more happiness, Misery attracts more misery.

Change your thoughts. Change your life,
Life is basically very simple, People make it complicated. Choose to be happy.
You only have one life, Choose happiness.

A Few More Poems to Keep you Inspired

Special moments

I heard the bird singing at twenty past four, So I turned the key and opened the door,
I couldn't see it but I knew it was there,
As it sang it's pure song in the cold morning air.

Then silence returned as I made a cup of tea, The bird had thrown and left the tree,
One sweet moment but it had soon passed, It reminded me that nothing will last.

It is therefore important to take a day at a time, This has always been a philosophy of mine,
To enjoy each moment, and to look for the good in every day,
By being grateful more special moments will come your way.

Change Your Words Change Your Life

LOOKING ON THE BRIGHT SIDE OF LIFE

Try to be positive in all that you do,
Keep looking on the bright side, and the sun will come shining through,
Look for the good and make sure you smile at least once a day
Then you will gain more happiness, and your fears will just drift away.

If your thoughts are negative, you will be sad, If your thoughts are positive you will be glad,
Why would you want to keep a negative frame of mind?

When you can be positive, happy, loving and kind.
By changing your thoughts, you can change your life too.
Keep looking for the good in all that you do, What you think about expands in your mind,
So, think positive thoughts and leave your fears behind

A Few More Poems to Keep you Inspired

THE BLESSING

I bless you with light and love,
I bless you with guidance from above,
I bless you with kindness, laughter and a beaming smile,
I bless you with passion to go the extra mile.

I bless you with happiness, joy and peace,
I bless you with a serenity that will never cease,
I bless you with courage to achieve all your dreams,
I bless you with some silence and all that it means.

I bless you with intuition that will show you the way,
I bless you with finding goodness in every day.
I bless you with the desire to be the very best you can be.
I bless you with finding answers from within, for that is the key.

Change Your Words Change Your Life

HAPPINESS

When the day is done, and nothing has gone right,
turn your thoughts back to a time of delight.
Recall how wonderful some days can be,
then focus your mind on a special day that was amazing to see.

When things go wrong as they sometimes will, don't be thinking you are "over the hill",
think of a time when success came your way,
By focusing on good moments, more will come to stay.

So, switch your thoughts and turn on the light,
Thinking happy thoughts will make you feel bright,
Since happiness can bring you peace of mind.
By focusing on happiness, this is what you will find.

A Few More Poems to Keep you Inspired

THE BEST MEDICINE

Fun, free and easy to use,
Will help you far more than wine and booze, Boosts your energy and can reduce your pain,
Increase your happiness, and will help keep you sane.

Relaxes muscles and protects your heart, Binds people together, and is easy to start,
Can enhance relationships, and improves your mood,
Try not to do it, though, when eating food.

Promotes group bonding, and adds joy to your life,
Helps you cope with stress, anxiety and strife,
Strengthens the immune system, and starts with a smile, Eases your fears, and doubts for a while.

Laughter is the best medicine they say, Try it more often it will improve your day.

Change Your Words Change Your Life

The Key To Happiness

The key to happiness is to be happy now,
Even if you are struggling try to focus on happiness somehow,
It is vital to your future, and please believe me it's true,
Your future will not be brighter if you are always feeling blue.

To see the future be it now, and it will make you smile, Think happiness now, and you can go the extra mile,

Your current thoughts must be happy, and you must be grateful too,
Your future will be brighter, if you let the sun keep shining through.

Please try to focus on happiness each and every day,
Make it a habit to be happy and positive in every way,

A Few More Poems to Keep you Inspired

By thinking happiness to brighten your day,
Develop the happiness habit, and believe me it will stay.

Other Poems

THE JOURNEY

I've been to the moon and back, and followed all the stars,
A journey around the Universe, including Jupiter and Mars,
There were no restrictions on this journey,
I just floated through the air,
It was as if I was in a trance, but I clearly didn't care,
It was a special journey, and I achieved all my dreams, And then I realised that life is not always what it seems.

Coming back home I knew I had to change,
Life is moving on, and now it's time to turn the page,
I need and I have started to make a clearer space,
It's full of light and love, a truly amazing place.

Other Poems

I am throwing out all my doubts and fears,

And replacing them with happiness and not tears,

Our lives are created by the thoughts in our minds,

All answers can be found within, "So seek and you will find".

IS THIS JUST ME

I want to sing like a blackbird high in a tree, I want to smell the blossom I want to be,
I want to soar like an eagle, and hum like a bee, Is this just me?

I want to be free of doubts and happy all the time,
I want to change forever, and I want to be happy and kind,
Is this just me?

I want to be grateful for every moment of my life,
Including the pain, the stress and the strife,
I want to learn from the good and the bad, I want to seek wisdom and never be sad, Is this just me?

Other Poems

THE GAME OF LIFE

Back to the drawing board, Life is such a game,
You win some, you lose some, But in the end, it's all the same.

Follow your bliss, follow your heart,
It doesn't matter if you make a false start, Be on purpose and give yourself a chance, Otherwise, life will lead you a merry dance.

Focus your mind on where you want to be, Keeping away negative thoughts is always the key,
Believe you can succeed, and you can climb to the top,
But don't forget to smell the roses before the dancing stops.

Change Your Words Change Your Life

BEING GRATEFUL.

I am grateful for having a roof over my head,
I am grateful for the mattress, so I can sleep on my bed, I am grateful for a walking stick to help me to walk,
I am grateful for my voice, so I can talk.

I am grateful for the stars and the moon,
I am grateful for the knife, the fork and the spoon. I am grateful for my car, so I can travel around,
I am grateful for my ears, so I can hear the silence and the sound.

I am grateful for my eyes, that give me my sight,
I am grateful for the days, that turn darkness into light, I am grateful to be able to laugh, or even cry,
I will continue to be grateful, until the day I die.

Other Poems

PENCIL POWER.

I can write a poem to make you laugh or cry, I can write out my will, for when I die,
I can rub out what's wrong, when I make a mistake, I can write down a recipe for a chocolate cake.

I can make a plan for the day ahead, I can write a song that is in my head,
I can take down a message, when I answer the phone,
I can write down my goals when I am all alone.

I can write out my thoughts, in a diary each day, I can write a prayer, to help me to pray,
I can write out a shopping list, showing what I want for tea,

I can mark out the programmes I watch on TV.
I can sketch a robin, a wren or a dove,
For this is my pencil, a possession I love.

Change Your Words Change Your Life

BUFFY.

Buffy was a special dog and she knew it too,
She was loved by everyone, not just me and you,
Buffy got excited, when getting ready for a walk, She was a very clever dog, who could almost talk.

Buffy was well loved, and looked after in style,
She was such a playful dog and could almost make you smile,
Buffy had a short life, she was only eight, But there were many memories to celebrate.

I only met Buffy once, she was excited and ready to go, A dog full of life, but little did we know,
Buffy gave so much pleasure and unconditional love,
She is at peace now, and resting in Heaven above.

KINDNESS

Try to be kind in all that you do
You will feel better for it and happier too Hold open a door or give a beautiful smile
Give a homeless person a sandwich, just go the extra mile
It will give you peace of mind and make your life worthwhile
It benefits your health and reduces your stress
Just be kind for no reason and not to impress
Give someone a helping hand, it will improve your mood too
For all acts of kindness will come back to you
Kindness slows down the aging process. Believe me it's true
Send a friend a box of chocolates or flowers too
Give someone an honest compliment and they will appreciate you
Just try to be kind in all that you do.

Ho'oponopono

Ho'oponopono is a Hawaiian healing practice based on forgiveness and reconciliation. In 1976 Mormah Simeona, who was regarded as a healing priest, adopted the traditional method, Ho'oponopono.

This involves the method of mutual forgiveness within the family .She later extended it to deal with general problem solving, and to spiritual self help healing.

Her version was influenced by Christianity, and by her studies in China and India. A company called Pacifica Seminars which was founded by Mormah Simeona, started teaching the Ho'oponpono seminars in Germany. Other seminars were held on a regular basis in Poland, France and Denmark.

After she died in 1992 her former student Ihaleakala Dr, Hew Len wrote a book with Joe Vitale called Zero Limits. The practice of Ho'oponopono involves using a mantra using the following words, "I'm sorry. Please forgive me. Thank you. I love you." It is based

Ho'oponopono

on taking complete responsibility not only for our own actions, but for everyone else in our lives.

Another source of practising Ho'oponopono is the book on haiku poems.

This ancient healing system is a method of forgiveness, and an aid to self love and balance.

The repetition of the mantra "I am sorry. Please forgive me. Thank you. I love you." is said to allow the programming of the subconscious mind for healing purposes.

When you say the words in the mantra it helps get rid of negativity within you, and by chanting the Ho'oponopono, you will find it comforting as it helps you discover security and comfort yourself with forgiveness and love.

Ho'oponopono helps to develop forgiveness, love and harmony to difficult relationships, and can bring relief and healing. Although it is a simple method, the mantra is seen to be effective medicine for the soul, and it is definitely worth a try, as by using the four short sentences it can help transform your thinking patterns. The mantra which is known as the Ho'oponopono prayer can also be used to attract money.

Change Your Words Change Your Life

You can say it out allowed or silently, and if you say it with belief, it can help with the healing process, it can be repeated as many times as you feel is necessary throughout the week.

Ho;oponopono means to 'set right', and in this case setting things by acknowledging your responsibility for having caused wrong, seeking forgiveness and love, and finally expressing gratitude .

There are four steps to be done within your own mind, and it does not require participation in a group, but at the same time, practicing the mantra in a group will help bring about a more collective spiritual togetherness.

The four steps are :

1) Take responsibility.

2) Ask forgiveness.

3) Send love.

4) Thank you.

For it to become more effective I cannot overemphasize the value of using the mantra as much as possible, especially when you have unresolved issues that need your attention.

I try to say the mantra myself every morning, but whatever time you want to use is of course down to your own preference. Dr. Hew Len is now fully retired, but is still alive and well.

Ho'oponopono practitioners refer to the practice of the mantra as 'cleaning', which helps to eliminate negative feelings, and to erase negativity that is blocking you from resolving current issues or problems.

There are courses that you can do online to become a Certified Ho'oponopono practitioner.

There are also quite a number of books written on the subject, such as 'The Book of Ho'oponopono, The Hawaiian Practice of Forgiveness and Healing' by Luc Bodmin, 'At Zero Limits' by Joe Vitale and Dr.Len Hew, and 'The Ancient Hawiian practice of gratitude and forgiveness', by Carol Berger.

You can also find out more about Ho'oponopono on YouTube or Google.

I would like to refer you to a beautiful Ho'oponopono song on YouTube called the Ho'oponopono Song sung by Arnan Ryusuke Seto.

My sister God love her, loved this song, and we used to sing along to it sometimes in the house, or in the car on the way home from a trip out.

Ho'oponopono - Blue Water

This is a method of enhancing the quality of water by filling a blue glass coloured bottle with ordinary tap water, providing the tap water is normally of a standard that is fit to drink without boiling.

Once the bottle has been filled, it needs to be placed outside in direct sunlight, and left out all day, so that the sun's rays can penetrate through the bottle and energise the water.

Drinking this water can produce a calming effect, and can help to relax your mind, and can gently help to remove your worries.

The colour blue is said to help with communication, regeneration and sleep and is used to treat a variety of conditions, such as high blood pressure, stress, and headaches.

It aids meditation and spiritual growth because of its calming effect.

Ho'oponopono

Blue is the colour associated with the throat chakra, which is related to the expression of one's self, and creativity.

By drinking the water from the blue bottle that has been exposed to sunlight' it is said to help and empower the throat chakra. On a physical level, a weakened throat chakra can cause sore throats, nervous coughing, laryngitis, and hoarseness

Apparently if you spray it on your plants, it can help them grow.

It is also said it will help in a gentle way, to change the mental patterns that are created in your life that you do not want or need anymore.

As you will gather I am very impressed with this healing technique, and although everyone must do their own research, and make up their own mind about the possible benefits, the poem I wrote about Ho'oponopono reflects my thoughts and feelings about this healing method, Ho'oponopono.

Change Your Words Change Your Life

Ho'oponopono

"I'm sorry. Please forgive me. Thank you. I love you"
These are healing words believe me it's true,
When you find yourself thinking negative thoughts repeat these powerful words every day,

You will find improvements in your life, and in what you think and say.
It will help you release more negative memories, and bring more peace of mind,
You will find yourself calmer now, with less sadness and doubts of every kind,

By practicing this daily, this will reduce your stress, and help with anxiety to,
There are Ho'oponopono prayers and songs, whatever you prefer to do.
It might seem very strange, depending upon your point of view,
But this is a powerful technique that is well worth looking into,

Ho'oponopono

It is practiced daily around the world, they are such simple words, but positive to,
"I'm sorry. Please forgive me. Thank you. I love you"

We are all on a journey, and we are all travelling on different paths. I hope this book will help you, or guide you to discover more about yourself, and will give you a little more insight into your chosen route to success, health, wealth and happiness, or whatever you desire.

Thank you for reading it and God bless you all.

David Prior

Printed in Great Britain
by Amazon